This Book Belongs To

_____

Easy Planners And Journals
To help you organize your life

This book is copyright protected. Reproducing this book is prohibited and not allowed without the permission of the author. All rights reserved.